OBEY THE SABBATH: REST IN CHRIST

A. Blake White

Published by Canon Sense
canonsense.com
Cover Design by Thread Rocket

Other Books by A. Blake White

The Newness of the New Covenant
The Law of Christ: A Theological Proposal
Galatians: A Theological Interpretation
Abide in Him: A Theological Interpretation of John's First Letter
Union with Christ: Last Adam & Seed of Abraham
What is New Covenant Theology? An Introduction
Theological Foundations for New Covenant Ethics
The Abrahamic Promises in the Book of Galatians
Missional Ecclesiology
The Imitation of Jesus
Joyful Unity in the Gospel
God's Chosen People
The Five Solas

For Alicia. Thank you for your selfless love and unwavering support. You are God's greatest earthly gift to me.

TABLE OF CONTENTS

Chapter 1

Introduction

~

The Sabbath has been a hot topic of debate among Bible-believing Christians for centuries. In many ways, the heat hasn't cooled. In some circles, the water is boiling. This is one of those theological areas that has significant practical and pastoral implications and applications. It is important that we get it right.

The Sabbath commandment is also a great test case for how we do theology. Our views on the Sabbath are determined by our hermeneutic, by how we relate the Old Testament and New Testament, by how we relate systematic theology and biblical theology, by our posture toward extrabiblical documents, by where we place final authority, and whether or not we truly and consistently let exegesis be the lifeblood of theology.

Pastorally, will we bind consciences with human tradition? Will we require members to work six days? Will we require meals to be prepared on Saturday? Will we forbid recreation on Sunday? Or will we preach the freedom Christ brings in the gospel? Will we point our people to the only place true Sabbath rest is to be found?

Chapter 2

Theological Systems

~

As mentioned in the introduction, our view of the Sabbath will largely be determined by our hermeneutic. In other words, often our theological presuppositions undergird and guide our exegesis of passages on the Sabbath, sometimes unknowingly. Within Evangelicalism, there are three main theological systems that attempt to make sense of the big picture of Scripture: Covenant Theology, New Covenant Theology, and Dispensationalism.[1] There are variations of each system and

---

[1] See Peter J. Gentry and Stephen J. Wellum, *Kingdom Through Covenant: A Biblical-Theological Understanding of the Covenants* (Wheaton, IL: Crossway

there is diversity within each system, but all Christians will land in one of these three camps, even if they have never heard of them. Simply asking a few questions about the Law, the Sabbath, Israel, and baptism will demonstrate this.

So, this is an "in-house debate," a conversation among friends who are united by so many wonderful truths, with a high view of Scripture undergirding them all. Those with a low view of Scripture do not have these types of conversations. Sometimes we need to be reminded of all we agree on as we discuss and debate differences.[2]

Books, 2012), 39-80 for a helpful overview of the varieties of Dispensationalism and Covenant Theology. For a critical analysis of both, see John G. Reisinger, *Abraham's Four Seeds: A Biblical Examination of the Presuppositions of Covenant Theology and Dispensationalism* (Frederick, MD: New Covenant Media, 1998).

[2] For example, for the blurb on Richard Barcellos' critique of New Covenant Theology, Sam Waldron writes, "There is no greater danger to historic, Reformed Christianity today than the assault on its emphasis on the Law of God . . . The rampant antinomian attack on this great doctrine threatens the very foundations of biblical Christianity . . . This book mounts a devastating counterattack on one of the most subtle and dangerous attacks on the Reformed doctrine of the law of God," Richard Barcellos, *In Defense of the Decalogue : A Critique of New Covenant Theology* (Enumclaw, WA: Winepress Publishing, 2001). This type of rhetoric borders on the absurd. Every New Covenant Theologian I know affirms the inerrancy of Scripture, the doctrines of grace, the five *solas*, complementarianism, believer's baptism, biblical church membership and discipline, and a commitment to expositional preaching, to name just a few key areas of agreement. Sam and his ilk need to get out more or simply read anything on the best seller list at their local Christian bookstore. Richard Barcellos' tone and posture is

I am exegetically persuaded that New Covenant Theology is the biblical-theological system that is most faithful to the Canon of Scripture. We also argue that it is the most consistently Christ-centered way of putting the Canon together. Though there is some diversity on secondary issues within New Covenant Theology, and some prefer the label "Progressive Covenantalism,"[3] every adherent I know agrees on the following seven essentials:[4]

- There is one plan of God centered in Jesus Christ

- The Old Testament should be interpreted in

---

exemplary in *Getting the Garden Right* (Cape Coral, FL: Founders Press, 2019), 28.

[3] Stephen J. Wellum and Brent E. Parker say that "progressive covenantalism" is a subset of New Covenant Theology, *Progressive Covenantalism: Charting a Course between Dispensational and Covenantal Theologies* (Nashville: B&H Academic, 2016), 2 (cf. 70 n. 2, 73, 111). In *Kingdom Through Covenant,* Gentry and Wellum say that progressive covenantalism fits "broadly under the umbrella of what is called 'new covenant theology'", 24 (cf. 80 n. 119). While some bloggers want to make these two movements entirely different systems, the history will not allow it. E.g., many of the early and current published writers on New Covenant Theology affirm a covenant with creation as well as the imputation of Christ's active obedience.

[4] These are briefly explained in my book, *What Is New Covenant Theology? An Introduction* (Frederick, MD: New Covenant Media, 2012).

light of the New Testament

- The Old Covenant was temporary by divine design

- The Old Covenant Law is a unit

- Christians are not under the Law of Moses, but the law of Christ

- All members of the New Covenant community are fully forgiven and indwelt by the Holy Spirit

- The church is the eschatological Israel via union with Israel's Messiah

Although there are other essential differences between Dispensationalism and New Covenant Theology, we largely agree on the question of the Sabbath.[5] Therefore,

---

[5] However, we also arrive at our conclusions from different avenues. Our view of the storyline of Scripture is *very* different. So, when Jim Renihan calls New Covenant Theology "a radical form of Dispensationalism," he shows his ignorance of the details of both systems, *1689 Federalism Compared to New Covenant Theology & Progressive Covenantalism*, accessed December 24, 2019, https://www.youtube.com/watch?v=_Uq_S3-HjRo. Besides opposing storylines, the heart of the differences between New Covenant Theology and Dispensationalism revolve around our views of Israel. For *a* New Covenant take on Israel, see my book *God's Chosen People* (Colorado Springs: Cross to Crown, 2017).

I will limit my engagement to Covenant Theology. Though there are important differences between Presbyterians and Baptist Covenant Theology, on the question of the Sabbath, there is substantial agreement. Let me rush to affirm how much I love these brothers and sisters. I love their Reformational heritage, much of their confessions, their large view of God, and their high view of Scripture. I put the five *solas* on my groom cake.[6] I share affinity with these theologians much more than many within my own denomination, the Southern Baptist Convention, which all too often is pragmatically-driven. I tried hard to become Presbyterian in college. I figured being a PCA or OPC elder would be much nicer fit than a Southern Baptist pastor. The Bible wouldn't let me. When I learned of the Founders Ministry, I was elated. That is, until I attended a regional conference and realized I was an unwelcome guest due to my views on the Sabbath. I value so much of what my Covenant Theologian brothers and friends stand for, but think they are wrong on the issue of the Sabbath, which shows the larger differences in the way we read the storyline of Scripture. To understand the origins of Covenant Theology, we must consider a few historic confessions.

----

[6] See A. Blake White, *The Five Solas* (Colorado Springs: Cross to Crown, 2019).

Chapter 3

A Word About Confessions

~

Covenant Theology, as we know it, is solidly codified in the Westminster Confession of Faith and its derivative, the Second London Baptist Confession of Faith. These confessions teach that history is structured around three primary covenants: the covenant of redemption before creation, the covenant of works with Adam in the garden, and the covenant of grace.[7] It is important to realize

---

[7] There is debate among 1689ers about the covenant of grace. See Pascal Denault, *The Distinctiveness of Baptist Covenant Theology* (Birmingham: Solid Ground Christian Books, 2013). 1689 Federalism attempts to show that the substance of the covenant of grace is not in

that these covenants are not found in Scripture. They are man-made, eisegetically-derived. In other words, they are *theological* rather than *exegetically* established. New Covenant Theologians obnoxiously insist on using Scripture's own categories and language whenever possible, which is the vast majority of the time. The danger among the majority of adherents of Covenant Theology is to flatten out the covenants and miss the discontinuity, especially with regards to the newness of the new covenant. The new covenant is not merely a renewed administration of the covenant of grace. It is *new*.[8] King Jesus and the gift of the Spirit bring qualitative newness.

Covenant Theology holds that there is a tripartite distinction within the Old Covenant Law. According to their theological approach, there are moral aspects, ceremonial aspects, and civil aspects. They see the ceremonial and civil aspects fulfilled in Christ and no longer binding on New Covenant Christians. The moral law, however, is eternally binding. For them, this primarily means the Decalogue, which of course includes the fourth command (see the Westminster Confession of Faith XIX,

---

the garden, but is the new covenant. Richard Barcellos contends that the Second London Baptist Confession and the Westminster Confession are on the same page theological regarding the covenant of works, even though different language is used, *Getting the Garden Right*, 38-52. I obviously don't have a dog in that fight.

[8] A. Blake White, *The Newness Of The New Covenant* (Frederick, MD: New Covenant Media, 2007).

XXI and Second London Baptist Confession XIX, XXII). This makes sense if the Old Covenant and the New Covenant are merely differing administrations of the same ole covenant of grace.

One can appreciate the candidness of Covenant Theologian John Frame, when he writes, "Our threefold distinction, though not found explicitly in Scripture, is a useful tool to analyze the various laws in the Bible."[9] It is useful until it isn't. It is useful until it causes skewed exegesis. When it comes to binding the consciences of the people of God, shouldn't we limit our teaching to that which is found explicitly in Scripture? He goes on to lay out his cards. In cases where moral and ceremonial categories are not so helpful, he says, "We don't determine that a law is ceremonial and therefore not currently normative; rather, we follow the reverse procedure. Rather than determining that a law is abrogated because it is ceremonial, we determine that it is ceremonial because we believe it to be abrogated. So, *moral* is just a label for those laws we believe to be currently normative, rather than a quality of the laws that leads us to that conclusion. The same is true for the label *ceremonial*. There is nothing particularly wrong with this procedure, as long as we understand what we are doing."[10] I think there is much wrong with this procedure. This

---

[9] John M. Frame, *The Doctrine of the Christian Life*, First edition. (Phillipsburg, N.J: P & R Publishing, 2008), 214.

[10] Ibid.

renowned Covenant Theologian admits that something besides exegesis is driving this bus. These distinctions come out of thin air. More accurately, they come from the Confession undergirding the exegete's presuppositions. We will say more about the lack of biblical evidence for the supposed tripartite division in the next chapter.

These confessions also teach that the Sabbath, the seventh day, was transferred to Sunday, the first day. The Second London Baptist Confession of Faith of 1689 states "After the resurrection of Christ it was changed to the first day of the week, which is called the Lord's Day."[11] The proof texts are 1 Corinthians 16:1-2, Acts 20:7, and Revelation 1:10, all of which mention the first day, but none of which say anything about the Sabbath. Only Revelation 1:10 calls it "the Lord's day." There is not an exegetical shred of evidence for transferring the Sabbath to the first day of the week. This comes from human tradition, not the exegesis of texts.

Notice I have only mentioned the *Second* London Baptist Confession so far. There was a first one, which was not as comprehensive and became hard to find not too long after its printing. It is important to understand why the Second London Baptist Confession was adopted.[12] With

---

[11] Stan Reeves, ed., *The 1689 Baptist Confession of Faith in Modern English* (Cape Coral, Florida: Founders Press, 2017), XXII:7, 46.

[12] Gary D. Long, *The First London Confession of Faith, 1646 Edition: With an Appendix by Benjamin Cox* (Belton, TX: Sovereign Grace Ministries,

King Charles II at the helm, there was persecution and harsh restrictions for dissenters due to the Clarendon Code of 1661 adopted by the pro-Anglican Parliament. The Conventicle Act of 1664 prohibited anyone six years old and up from gathering for worship at any service other than those approved by the Church of England. In 1665, the Five Mile Act required the dissenters to swear that they would not rebel against the king or his government, or they would be exiled. Charles approved the Act of Uniformity in 1662. The Church of England wanted uniformity of religion. The churches of that time period wanted toleration and Baptists needed people to know they were good sound Protestants like the Presbyterians and Congregationalists and not crazy like the extreme wing of the Anabaptists and the Quakers. The so-called dissenters needed to show doctrinal unity, so the Congregationalists followed the larger body of Presbyterians, who had ruled under Cromwell, and the Particular Baptists followed the Congregationalists in order to show a unified front. The Congregationalists adopted an adapted version of the Westminster Confession of Faith (1646) in 1658 in the Savoy Declaration. The

2003), viii-ix; Thomas K. Ascol, *From the Protestant Reformation to the Southern Baptist Convention: What Hath Geneva to Do with Nashville*, 2nd edition. (Cape Coral, FL: Founders Press, 2013), 26-27; Heather A. Kendall, *One Greater Than Moses: A History of New Covenant Theology* (Orange, California.: Quoir, 2016), 43-44; William L. Lumpkin, *The Story of Baptist Confessions of Faith* (Louisville: The Southern Baptist Theological Seminary, 1957), 12; W.J. McGlothlin, *Baptist Confessions of Faith* (Philadelphia: American Baptist Publication Society, 1911), 216-17; W.L. Lumpkin, *Baptist Confessions of Faith* (Valley Forge: Judson Press, 1974), 235-40.

Baptists met in London in 1677 to edit the Westminster Confession to fit their credobaptist theology, changing it on the church, polity, sacraments, and religious liberty.[13]

Tom Ascol writes, "The framers of this *Second London Confession* did not regard themselves as moving away from that which had been affirmed in the 1644 Confession. In fact, they observed that the *Westminster* (1646) and *Savoy* (1658) actually followed the same theological convictions as the earlier Baptist Confession – not at every point, obviously, but certainly on the main issues."[14] Granted, both the First and Second London Confessions are Baptistic and Calvinistic, but there are significant differences that ought not be minimized.[15] It all depends on how one defines "the

---

[13] See "A Tabular Comparison of the 1646 Westminster Confession of Faith, the 1658 Savoy Declaration of Faith, the 1677/1689 London Baptist Confession of Faith and the 1742 Philadelphia Confession of Faith," accessed January 4, 2020, https://www.proginosko.com/docs/wcf_sdfo_lbcf.html.

[14] Ascol, *From the Protestant Reformation to the Southern Baptist Convention*, 27.

[15] Reformed Baptist Jon English Lee admits that article XXV of the First London Confession "appears to be contradicting the role of the law as necessary for faith that had previously been articulated," but that wouldn't fit the needed narrative so the "terrors of the law" are reinterpreted to fit the Second London Baptist Confession, which in his mind "represents the most significant advance in the articulation of Baptist beliefs regarding the doctrine of the Moral Law of God to date," "The Moral Law of God and Baptist Identity," *Founders Journal* 94 (Fall 2013). Baptists in America adopted the Second London in the form of

main issues."

The First London Confession of Faith of 1646 was first published by seven particular Baptist churches in London in 1644. John Spilsbury may have been the chief architect of the statement, with the help of William Kiffin, Samuel Richardson and Benjamin Cox, but we cannot be sure. It was revised two years later to clarify statements, strengthen its Calvinistic outlook, and re-word parts about baptism after responses were written, especially that of Daniel Featley in *The Dippers Dipt*. Part of the reason for the confession was to separate the Particular Baptists from the Anabaptists as well as the Arminian General Baptists.[16] An

---

the Philadelphia and Charleston Confessions. Tellingly, in the 1798 annual circular letter to the churches of the Philadelphia Baptist Association, we read this: "The compilers of our Confession of faith were desirous to use the same language with other Christians, as far as was thought consistent with a good conscience; and it may be, on this subject, they conformed more than can be supported by the Holy Scriptures, or any arguments justly drawn from by the Holy Scriptures, or any arguments justly drawn from them" in John G. Reisinger, *In Defense of Jesus, the New Lawgiver* (Frederick, MD: New Covenant Media, 2008), 287.

[16] "The title of the original Confession of 1646 was: 'A Confession of Faith of Seven Congregations or Churches of Christ in London, Which are Commonly (But Unjustly) Called Anabaptists'," David H. Wenkel, ed., *The London Baptist Confession of 1646: A Modern Version for the Church Today* (Greenville, SC: Ambassador International, 2017), 15; *Baptist Confessions, Covenants, and Catechisms,* eds. Timothy and Denise George (Nashville: B&H, 1996), 34; Barry Hamlin Howson, "A Historical and Comparative Study of the First and Second London Baptist Confessions of Faith with Reference to the Westminster and Savoy Confessions"

influential, anonymous tract warning London about the crazy Münster Anabaptists was spread around so the Particular Baptists needed to distance themselves from the anarchy. They did so with this uniquely Baptistic Confession. I contend that they had it right the first time.[17] For our purposes, most importantly, the First London Baptist Confession is not structured around Covenant Theology. It contains no command to keep the Sabbath and does not advocate a tripartite distinction of the Law. Its focus is decidedly Christ-centered. The call is not to obey the Law of Moses, but to "presseth after a heavenly and evangelical obedience to all the commands, which Christ as head and king in His new covenant hath prescribed to them."[18] I have to wonder if those who try to conflate these Confessions have given them a careful reading.[19]

(M.A., McGill University (Canada), 1996), 13-14; Lumpkin, *The Story of Baptist Confessions of Faith*, 5; Lumpkin, *Baptist Confessions of Faith*, 145.

[17] Baptist historian W.J. McGlothlin writes of the 1646 Confession: "It is perhaps the most independent of the Baptist Confessions, and is one of the noblest productions ever put forth by them. It probably still represents the views of the Baptists of the world more nearly than any other single Confession," *Baptist Confessions of Faith*, 170. See Richard P. Belcher and Tony Mattia, *A Discussion of Seventeenth Century Baptist Confessions of Faith* (Columbia, SC: Richbarry Press, 1983) for an argument that the two confessions share the same theology of law.

[18] *The First London Confession of Faith, 1646 Edition*, XXIX, 11-12.

[19] McGlothlin writes of the Second Confession: "They affirm the agreement of this Confession in substance with that of 1644; but, as a matter of fact, there are differences of considerable scope and

Here is the take-away: it seems that the Particular Baptists adopted a Presbyterian Confession for pragmatic reasons. Persecution caused them to adopt what the Presbyterians and Congregationalists had written. They "baptized" a Confession with a substructure that undergirds infant baptism, namely Covenant Theology. Had there been no push towards uniformity, it is unlikely that the Baptists would have adopted a Presbyterian Confession. However, even for those who remain committed to the view that both Confessions teach Covenant Theology, Scripture reigns supreme. God's Word is the norming norm. We are committed to *Sola Scriptura*. This does not mean we downplay history or jettison all Confessions; it just means that Scripture trumps tradition full stop.

---

importance. After a careful reading of the former, one feels himself almost in a new world in this. There are striking phrases and other reminiscences of the former Confession, but in the main all is changed," *Baptist Confessions of Faith,* 216-17; Lumpkin similarly writes, "As a matter of fact, there are numerous and marked differences between this Confession and that of 1644," *Baptist Confessions of Faith,* 237. The First is Christ-focused, the Second is structured around Covenant Theology.

Chapter 4

An Inconsistency and an Irony

~

Before we begin our exegetical journey, let me mention an inconsistency and an irony. As a New Covenant Theologian, I have received a fair bit of criticism regarding the Sabbath. I, and other New Covenant guys, have often been called "antinomians," that is, those who are against (*anti*) the Law (*nomos*) of God. I confess frustration at inconsistency among Covenant Theologians. They will rabidly argue for the validity of the Sabbath commandment on paper, then live just like I do on Sundays. I am glad they enjoy the freedom for which Christ set us free (Gal 5:1, 13), but they need to either align their lives with their theology, or their theology with their lives. The vast majority that I know work, watch sports, mow the grass, go out to eat, cook, and watch the NFL on Sundays. But *I am the antinomian!?*

The Second London Baptist Confession is quite clear and specific. It says, "The Sabbath is kept holy to the Lord when people have first prepared their hearts appropriately and arranged their everyday affairs in advance. Then they observe a holy rest all day from their works, words and thoughts about their secular employment and recreation. Not only that, but they also fill the whole time with public and private acts of worship and the duties of necessity and mercy."[20] I would humbly but boldly ask my Covenant Theologian brothers, do you work on Sundays? Does your wife cook on Sundays? Do you recreate? Do you work out? Do you start a fire (Exod 35:3)? Do you *actually* care about keeping the Sabbath holy or just arguing theology in order to defend a historic Confession?

About ten years ago, my wife and I were in a new city and were not yet in full time ministry. We looked around for like-minded churches that we could join. We found one, but upon further investigation, I found that they held to a Sabbatarian confession of faith. At the time, my

---

[20] Reeves, *The 1689 Baptist Confession of Faith in Modern English*. I might add that the New Hampshire Confession and Abstract of Principles is Sabbatarian as well.

wife Alicia was working one weekend a month as a nurse to help me get through graduate school. I called to talk to one of the pastors. "Hi, we are interested in visiting your church, but I noticed the article on keeping the Sabbath. My wife will have to work on one Sunday a month. Is that a problem?" The pastor replied, "Oh, no. Of course not, brother. I myself work at Starbucks on Sundays to supplement ministerial income." Click. What is the point of a confession if it is going to be readily dismissed? Would pastors do the same with adultery? Murder? Unlikely. Yet they are part of the same "eternal moral law of God."

Many churches who hold to Covenant Theology are faithful churches, holding forth the Word of Truth in all sorts of ways. Praise God. They are typically committed to expositional teaching. They usually practice the "missing mark" of a healthy church: church discipline.[21] If a church member is involved in unrepentant adultery, discipline will ensue. If a church member is involved in unrepentant lying, discipline will ensue. Unrepentant murder, discipline will ensue. Unrepentant stealing, discipline will ensue. I have never heard of a church member disciplined for breaking the Sabbath by a modern-day church that holds to Covenant Theology.[22] As noted, many of their pastors break

---

[21] Albert Mohler, "Discipline: The Missing Mark," in *Polity* ed. Mark Dever (Washington D.C.: 9 Marks Ministries, 2001), 43-56.

[22] I do know of some, who will discipline for perpetual non-attendance. My church would as well. But this is different than disciplining for performing works of employment or enjoyment on Sundays. My current

the Sabbath weekly. But on principle, there is *zero* moral difference between breaking the Sabbath and murder according to their theology. Both are part of the big ten. Both are contained in the Decalogue, the "eternal moral law of God." Ethically, they are on the exact same plane, but inconsistency abounds among Covenant Theologian pastors.

The irony I'd like to point out before we dive into Scripture is that when it comes to the Sabbath, Covenant Theology links hermeneutical arms with Dispensationalism.[23] They both betray a key hermeneutical principle: we must interpret the Old Testament as Christian disciples. They both take off their Christ-centered lenses, just at different points in their respective systems. Dispensationalists miss how Jesus transforms the land promise and the people of Israel. Covenant Theology misses how Jesus transforms the Sabbath. To that we now

---

church used to be consistent Sabbatarians. Read this newspaper clip: "According to historical records, members were disciplined regularly for attending street dances, dances in their homes, and playing baseball or fishing on Sunday! Losing one's temper was also reason for investigation and possible punishment. Guilty members could be restored to full membership if they apologized to the congregation for their misbehavior."

[23] John G. Reisinger hammers this point home again and again in *Abraham's Four Seeds* (Frederick, Md.: New Covenant Media, 1998), 5, 36, 47, 53, 58, 94, 99, 100, 118, as do Gentry and Wellum, *Kingdom Through Covenant,* 63, 69 n. 91, 76, 86, 113, 117-18, 122, 704 n. 115, 706 n. 121.

turn.

Chapter 5

Old Testament

~

The seventh day is significant from the earliest pages of Scripture. After each day, God has a closing formula of sorts:

- Genesis 1:5: "And there was evening and there was morning, the first day."

- Genesis 1:8: "And there was evening and there was morning, the second day."

- Genesis 1:13: "And there was evening and there was morning, the third day."

- Genesis 1:19: "And there was evening and there was morning, the fourth day."

- Genesis 1:23: "And there was evening and there was morning, the fifth day."

- Genesis 1:31: "And there was evening and there was morning, the sixth day."

Then God finishes and rests on the seventh day. God rests. There is no worship here, just God resting. There is no commandment here, just God resting. "So God blessed the seventh day and made it holy, because on it God rested from all his work that he had done in creation" (Gen 2:3). Why no closing formula like the other six days? Because the seventh day is open-ended. This is no accident. The seventh day is unlike the others. It is special. It is sanctified. And note that the first day is not special, the seventh day is special. "Sabbath" is not mentioned; only the seventh day. It is the way life is supposed to be lived. Adam and Eve and their progeny were supposed to live unending Sabbath life. The seventh day was left open-ended, for humanity to live the good life, resting with God in the garden-temple. In rabbinic Judaism, the new age was often described as "the world which is entirely Sabbath."[24]

---

[24] A.T. Lincoln, "Sabbath, Rest, and Eschatology in the New Testament," in D. A. Carson, *From Sabbath to Lord's Day: A Biblical, Historical and Theological Investigation* (Eugene, OR: Wipf & Stock, 2000), 199.

A case for Sabbath-keeping as a creation ordinance cannot be credibly established from these verses. It is simply not in these verses. New Testament scholar Tom Schreiner lists four reasons the Sabbath is *not* a creation ordinance.[25] First, if the Sabbath were a creation ordinance, the patriarchs would have been required to keep it. They were not. Second, not everything found in the creation narrative is mandatory for believers. Not all are required to farm land, for example. Third, since not everything in the creation narrative is mandated for believers, how would we determine what commands are applicable today? Fourth, the appeal to creation that we find in the Sabbath command functions as an analogy. The writer sees an analogy between God resting on the seventh day and the command for Israel to rest on the seventh day. I would add that if the Sabbath were a creation ordinance, the command would be clearly affirmed in the New Testament. As we will see, this is not the case. If one cannot prove from these verses that the Sabbath is a creation ordinance, the Sabbatarian view is undermined.

It is one thing to say that the seventh day of creation set the precedent and basis for the later commandment; It is

---

[25] Thomas R. Schreiner, "Goodbye and Hello: The Sabbath Commmand for New Coveant Believers," in Stephen J. Wellum and Brent E. Parker, eds., *Progressive Covenantalism: Charting a Course between Dispensational and Covenantal Theologies* (Nashville: B&H Academic, 2016), 168-170.

quite another to turn a foundation into a command. Christian teachers ought to have clear textual warrant to turn an indicative into an imperative. A command to obey the Sabbath is nowhere grounded in the created order.[26]

In fact, the first occurrence of the word "Sabbath" comes in Exodus 16. It is introduced in the context of Israel gathering manna (Exod 16:22-30). Sabbatarians argue that since this comes before the giving of the Law, it proves that the command is eternal. It does no such thing. Circumcision is commanded before the giving of the Law as well, but it is not an eternal command. Here in Exodus 16, the command was previously unknown to them, but God was training and preparing his people for the command that would come in Exodus 20. Exodus 16:29 says the Sabbath command was "given" to them. You do not give someone something they already possess.[27] Similarly, Nehemiah 9:13-14 is clear that the Sabbath was given with the giving of the Old Covenant: "You came down on Mount Sinai and spoke with them from heaven and gave them right rules and true laws, good statutes and commandments, and you made known to them

---

[26] A.G. Shead writes, "There is no mention of the Sabbath here, nor of rest. Instead we read of the 'seventh day' of creation, and of God 'ceasing' from his work. We should be careful not to read back into this passage more than it actually says," "Sabbath," in Brian S. Rosner, eds., *New Dictionary of Biblical Theology: Exploring the Unity Diversity of Scripture*, (Downers Grove, Ill: IVP Academic, 2000), 745.

[27] John G. Reisinger, *The Believer's Sabbath* (Frederick, MD.: New Covenant Media, 2002), 23.

your holy Sabbath and commanded them commandments and statutes and a law by Moses your servant."

Exodus 20:8-11 is the key passage: "Remember the Sabbath day, to keep it holy. Six days you shall labor, and do all your work, but the seventh day is a Sabbath to the LORD your God. On it you shall not do any work, you, or your son, or your daughter, your male servant, or your female servant, or your livestock, or the sojourner who is within your gates. For in six days the LORD made heaven and earth, the sea, and all that is in them, and rested on the seventh day. Therefore the LORD blessed the Sabbath day and made it holy."

Notice four oft-neglected aspects of this command. First, part of the command is to work six days. It seems like the American five-day work week ought to be rejected as ungodly by Covenant Theologians, rather than enjoyed like the rest of us. Second, this is a command about cessation from work, not worship. Third, this is a command not to work on Saturday. Sunday is not in view. What right do men think they have to change the Law of God? Seventh Day Adventists are actually more consistent Sabbatarians here. The Bible contains no "Sabbath transfer" theology. It was not until 330 AD that Sunday was called the Sabbath.[28]

---

[28] D. A. Carson, *From Sabbath to Lord's Day: A Biblical, Historical and Theological Investigation* (Eugene, OR: Wipf & Stock Pub, 2000), 282. Blomberg notes that Eusebius applied the pagan term "Sunday" to the first day of the week, but it was not until the 8th Century that Alcuin explicitly called Sunday the Christian Sabbath, *Perspectives on the Sabbath:*

There is no Sunday Sabbath keeping in the early church. Sabbath transfer theology is medieval and Thomistic, not patristic or apostolic.[29] Fourth, context shows this command is embedded in the "Book of the Covenant."[30] The command is one of the ten "words" (Exod 20:1), which are followed by the many "rules" of the Old Covenant (Exod 21:1). The rules are explications and applications of the words. Together, the ten words and many rules comprise what Moses calls the "Book of the Covenant" (Exod 24:7). "Moses came and told the people all the words of the LORD and all the rules" (Exod 24:3). The words and the rules are a package deal. The point being that it is arbitrary to pull the words from the rules since they belong together according to Moses. In sum, a tripartite division of the Old Covenant Law is foreign to the biblical worldview.[31] It does not arrive from exegesis but eisegesis.[32]

_____

Four Views, ed. Christopher John Donato (Nashville, TN: B&H Academic, 2011), 318

[29] See *Summa Theologica* 100.3-11.

[30] See Gentry and Wellum, *Kingdom Through Covenant,* 305-309, 355.

[31] Theonomy is actually more consistent. Seeing no explicit texts teaching the abolition of the so-called "civil" aspects of the Law, they claim that we should uphold both the "moral" and "civil" Old Covenant laws in the New Covenant era.

[32] One could make a better case that the Sabbath would land in the ceremonial category, rather than the moral. See the 1789 circular letter of the Philadelphia association found in Reisinger, *In Defense of Jesus, the New Lawgiver,* 284-291. Those Baptists argued the Sabbath command

Exodus 31:12-18 says that the Sabbath is a sign of the Old Covenant. Those who break it are to be put to death and cut off from Israel. Verse 14 says that to work physically is to defile the Sabbath. Israel is called to keep the sign, "as a covenant forever" (Exod 31:16), but this word "forever" means as long as the covenant lasts. It is perpetual for the duration of the covenant. As a sign, the Sabbath command lasts only as long as that covenant. The covenant of circumcision is described in the same way (Gen 17:7). The priesthood and its practices were often described with this word, "forever" (Exod 27:21, 28:43, 29:28, 30:21, 40:15, Lev 6:18, 6:22, 7:34, 7:36, 24:8 Num 18:19), yet no one today is advocating for a Levitical priesthood. It only lasted as long as the covenant. In sum, the Sabbath is the sign of the Old Covenant made with Israel. It is not too much to say that it is therefore the heart of the Old Covenant, but it is exactly that: the heart of the *Old* Covenant.

---

was not moral, but ceremonial, by which they meant commands that were "types or shadows of spiritual things, which might be abolished by the will of the legislator."

Chapter 6

Colossians 2

~

The message of the book of Colossians can be summarized as "Jesus + Nothing = Everything." Christ is our life. He is our all. He is all we need. He is sufficient. All things were created by him and for him (Col 1:16). He is to be preeminent. All this to say, he needs no supplement.

The gospel had gone to Colossae, likely through Epaphras, though I love the way the Apostle puts it. In Colossians 1:6, he says the gospel "has come to you, as indeed in the whole world it is bearing fruit and increasing." Today, we'd likely list the name of some catalytic plaid-wearing church planter in cuffed skinny jeans. Paul just says the gospel came. It is this message of the Messiah, crucified and risen, that came. Yeah, yeah, some guy named Epaphras came, but it is the message that makes the moves. It is the message that is bearing fruit and increasing, alluding back to the call of the first couple to be fruitful and multiply. The gospel is on the move, producing a new humanity around the New Man (Eph 2:15). The Word does the work. But not only that, this message that Jesus is sufficient, is also bearing fruit and increasing "among you." We grow by the gospel. More on that in a moment.

The church was started on the foundation of the sufficiency of Jesus, but they did not remain faithful. False teachers came in and distorted the purity of the gospel. Like most heresies, their teaching contained a mix of things. Their message contained a little paganism, a little mysticism, a little proto-Gnosticism, a little Judaism, and of course a little Jesus. If they had written one, their book surely would have made Oprah's book club. Paul counters the heresy by teaching about Jesus and his preeminence (Col 1:15-20).

He then warns them to continue in the faith they know, not shifting from the hope of the gospel of grace alone (Col 1:22-23). If they would reach maturity, it will be through the proclamation of Christ alone (Col 1:28-29). In him are hidden all the treasures of wisdom and knowledge, so there is no need to listen to those seeking to delude them with plausible arguments. No need to move on from Christ to man-made traditions, to the rules of men (Col 2:8, 20-

23). They should walk in Christ, just like they received him – through faith (Col 2:6).

Colossians 2:8 says, "See to it that no one takes you captive by philosophy and empty deceit, according to human tradition, according to the elemental spirits of the world, and not according to Christ." These false teachers are seeking to enslave the church by deceit and tradition, so Paul warns them: do not be taken captive by them to the elemental spirits of the world. What are those?[33] Put simply, the enslaving powers of darkness. Paul uses the phrase again in Colossians 2:20 when he says with Christ we have died to the elemental spirits of the world. We'll learn from Galatians that the principalities and powers will use anything, including the now obsolete Old Covenant Law, to make us drift from resting in Christ alone.

Now to the matter at hand. Colossians 2:16-17 says, "Therefore let no one pass judgment on you in questions of food and drink, or with regard to a festival or a new moon or a Sabbath. These are a shadow of the things to come, but the substance belongs to Christ." Those who try to claim that this is not the Jewish Sabbath are trying to catch air with a bug net. As Calvin put it, "Who but madmen cannot see what observance the apostle means?"[34] Paul lists the

---

[33] See my *The Law of Christ: A Theological Proposal* (Frederick, MD: New Covenant Media, 2010), 61-66.

[34] John Calvin, *Institutes of the Christian Religion,* ed. John T. McNeill, trans. For Lewis Battles (Louisville: Westminster John Knox

Jewish holy days: yearly, monthly, weekly.[35] Mark it down that God the Spirit through the Apostle Paul commands believers not to pass judgment on other believers with regard to the Sabbath command. I wish my Covenant Theology brothers would consider this command before throwing around the label "antinomian." We'll say more about that in the next chapter.

Paul says the Jewish calendar, including the Sabbath, is a shadow (*skia*) of what was to come, but the substance belongs to Christ. The author of Hebrews uses the same word: "For since the law has but a shadow of the good

---

Press,2006), 2.8.33, 399; See also Douglas Moo, *The Letters to the Colossians and to Philemon* (Grand Rapids: Eerdmans, 2008), 221-223; David W. Pao, *Colossians and Philemon* (Grand Rapids: Zondervan, 2012), 185

[35] Dick Lucas, *The Message of Colossians and Philemon* (Downers Grove, IL: IVP Academic, 1984), 113. Craig Blomberg, "The Sabbath as Fulfilled in Christ," in Christopher John Donato, ed. *Perspectives on the Sabbath,* 342-343. Blomberg writes, "No Colossian Christian of any ethnicity, knowing of Christianity's Jewish roots, having just had his or her attention drawn to a distinctively Jewish ritual, could hear Paul's words in verse 16 and reasonably deduce that he was thinking *only* of pagan holidays or special Jewish Sabbaths or certain parts of regular Jewish Sabbaths and not also of what Jews universally meant the overwhelming majority of the time when they used the word *Sabbath* without qualification. Could anyone be expected to conclude from this verse that Paul was in fact simultaneously implying the exact opposite of the straightforward language he used, something like 'but of course you must still observe the *Jewish* Sabbath or the *biblical parts* of the Sabbath or the *non-ceremonial* elements of the Sabbath'?"

things to come instead of the true form of these realities." The whole Old Covenant Law was a shadow, therefore of course the sign of that Old Covenant is also a shadow. The shadows point forward to the reality, to the substance. The word for substance here is *sōma,* which is often translated "body," which fits the shadow metaphor well. The Sabbath is just the shadow, but the shadow points to the real thing, the body, who is Christ Jesus.

So, don't go back to the shadow once the body is here. Why would you? It pointed forward to the things to come. Once those things come, there is no need to return.[36] It would be like me taking my kids to Disney World, passing the "50 Miles to Disney" sign, just to pull a U-turn in the Disney parking lot only to return to the "50 Miles to Disney" sign. Once I see that the shadow points to the substance, there is no need to return to the shadow.

If keeping the Sabbath was part of the eternal moral Law of God, Paul would have had to inform these Colossians. Rather, they are told not to let others judge them about it, since it pointed forward to Christ and his sufficiency. This verse clearly disproves Sabbatarianism.

---

[36] Moo writes, "Believers who belong to the new era through their incorporation into Christ therefore experience the reality to which the Old Testament and its law pointed. And they are no longer compelled to follow the laws of that earlier era," *Colossians,* 223.

Chapter 7

Romans 14

~

The book of Romans is the apex of Scripture. If you do not know Romans well, drop this book and begin reading and re-reading this great letter. As New Testament scholar F.F. Bruce put it, "There is no saying what may happen when people begin to study the letter to the Romans." Luther said, "This epistle is really the chief part of the New Testament and the very purest Gospel, and is worthy not only that every Christian should know it word for word, by heart, but occupy himself with it every day, as the daily bread of the soul. It can never be read or pondered too much, and the more it is dealt with the more precious it becomes, and the better it tastes."[37] Calvin said, "If we have gained a true understanding of this Epistle, we have an open door to all the most profound treasures of Scripture."[38] Stott said, "It is the fullest, plainest and grandest statement of the gospel in the New Testament."[39] J.I. Packer said all roads lead to Romans and called it the high peak of Scripture.[40] You get the point. Read it. Know it. Live it.

At the risk of oversimplification, Romans can be divided into four sections: the sinfulness of sin (1-3), the grace of God in the gospel (4-8), the sovereign plan of God (9-11), and the transforming power of the gospel (12-16). It is that last section that concerns us now. Romans 12:1 is a transitional verse from doctrine to life, from creed to deed, from indicative to imperative. If Romans 1-11 is true, and gloriously it is, how then shall we live? In light of these gospel mercies, we are to offer our whole selves to God in worship.

In Romans 14-15, Paul deals with disputable matters. Matters that ought not produce division and

---

[37] Martin Luther, *Commentary on Romans* (Grand Rapids: Kregel,1954), xiii.

[38] Quoted in John Stott, *The Message of Romans: God's Good News for the World* (Downers Grove, IL: IVP Academic, 2001), 19.

[39] Ibid.

[40] J.I. Packer, *Knowing God* (Downers Grove, IL: IVP, 1973), 253.

judgment, when rightly understood. There was disagreement and division within the church in Rome. I am glad we are past those days. This is not surprising since all of the churches addressed by the New Testament were fraught with tension as well. The dawning of the New Covenant and the passing of the Old was a challenging transition, especially for Jewish people. They were used to their customs. It's all they knew. In fact, it honored God! So, seeing Gentiles honor God without reference to the Old Covenant Law was hard. Judgment was the temptation.

Thus far in the letter, Paul has already made clear that New Covenant Christians are not bound to the Old Covenant Law. Romans 6:14 cannot be any clearer: "For sin will have no dominion over you, since you are not under law but under grace." Sometimes interpreters attempt to limit this to mean Christians are merely not under the penalty of the Law. Praise God, that is true, but this verse is saying more. We are not under the binding authority of the Law.[41] We are not under jurisdiction of the Law.[42] Christians

---

[41] Douglas J. Moo, "The Law of Moses or the Law of Christ," in John S. Feinberg, ed., *Continuity and Discontinuity: Perspectives on the Relationship Between the Old and New Testaments* (Wheaton, IL: Crossway, 1988), 211.

[42] Gentiles never were. Some argue that the authors of the New Testament often lump the Gentiles in with Israel. Israel was paradigmatic of the world. Their situation under the Old Covenant is paradigmatic of all people: sinful and unable. Gentiles share the plight of the Jews. Remember, Israel too, is in Adam. See Stephen Westerholm, *Perspectives Old and New on Paul* (Grand Rapids: Eerdmans, 2004), 302 n. 13, 333, 415-17; Douglas J. Moo, *The Epistle to the Romans* (Grand

are not under the realm of the Law, but under the realm of the new age inaugurated by the Last Adam (Rom 5:12-21).

Romans 7:4-6 is clear as well: "Likewise, my brothers, you also have died to the law through the body of Christ, so that you may belong to another, to him who has been raised from the dead, in order that we may bear fruit for God. For while we were living in the flesh, our sinful passions, aroused by the law, were at work in our members to bear fruit for death. But now we are released from the law, having died to that which held us captive, so that we serve in the new way of the Spirit and not in the old way of the written code." Jewish believers, "those who know the Law" (Rom 7:1), have died to the Old Covenant Law, released from that which held them captive. Paul is contrasting salvation-historical eras. New Covenant Christians serve in the age of the Spirit (New Covenant), not the age of the written code (Old Covenant). We are not under the Old Covenant therefore we are not bound to the sign of that covenant, the Sabbath.[43]

Rapids: Eerdmans, 1996), 151, 206, 388, 417, 449, 484 n. 66, 488; Douglas J. Moo, *Galatians* (Grand Rapids: Baker Academic, 2013), 168, 211-213, 221, 241, 249, 262, 267. I used to be more sympathetic to this view. See Brian S. Rosner *Paul and the Law* (Downers Grove, IL: IVP, 2013), 51-56.

[43] Thomas Schreiner, *40 Questions About Christians and Biblical Law* (Grand Rapids, MI: Kregel Academic, 2010), 212; Schreiner, "Good-bye and Hello," 164.

With that clear teaching in mind, consider Romans 14:1-4, which says, "As for the one who is weak in faith, welcome him, but not to quarrel over opinions. One person believes he may eat anything, while the weak person eats only vegetables. Let not the one who eats despise the one who abstains, and let not the one who abstains pass judgment on the one who eats, for God has welcomed him. Who are you to pass judgment on the servant of another? It is before his own master that he stands or falls. And he will be upheld, for the Lord is able to make him stand."

Paul calls the Jews "weak in faith." They should have known that the Old Covenant Law was not eternal. They should have known that a New Covenant was on its way (Jer 31:31-34, Ezek 36). They had seen Jesus, heard his teaching, believed his gospel, been instructed by the Apostles. So, when they looked down on those who did not keep the Old Covenant Law, they were showing weakness of faith. He specifically mentions the many food laws of the Old Covenant. Now they are mere opinions (Rom 14:1), not binding on the people of God. Jewish Christians can keep the food laws, or disregard the food laws. Whatever you do, do not pass judgment, because God hasn't. All good so far, since the food laws are supposedly classified as ceremonial, but such a distinction runs adrift in the next verses.

Romans 14:5-6 says, "One person esteems one day as better than another, while another esteems all days alike. Each one should be fully convinced in his own mind. The one who observes the day, observes it in honor of the Lord. The one who eats, eats in honor of the Lord, since he gives thanks to God, while the one who abstains, abstains in honor of the Lord and gives thanks to God." In a context with Jew/Gentile tensions about the Old Covenant Law, to suggest that Paul is not referring to the Jewish Sabbath in these verses is ludicrous. It is *the* day they would have thought of immediately.[44] And Paul relativizes it in one fell swoop. "Each one should be fully convinced in his own mind." Incredible. Just like the food laws, the Jewish calendar is not binding on New Covenant Christians. Keep the Sabbath or don't keep the Sabbath, just be sure about your decision and make sure you do not judge those who land differently. Do not pass judgment on your brother and do not despise him if he doesn't do what you prefer with regard to food and days (Rom 14:10, 13). Strikingly similar to Colossians 2, huh? The key is to walk in love toward one another (Rom 14:15). Rather than judging a brother or sister about food laws or Jewish days, "pursue what makes for peace and for mutual upbuilding" (Rom 14:19). The clear and plain teaching of this passage is that in the New Covenant, Christians do not have to obey the Sabbath command.

---

[44] Douglas J. Moo, *The Epistle to the Romans* (Grand Rapids: Eerdmans, 1996), 842.

Chapter 8

Galatians 4

~

Galatians can be broken down into three sections: autobiography (1:1-2:14), theology (2:15-4:31), and ethics (5:1-6:16). The Galatian Christians had a strong start, believing and living out the implications of faith alone in Christ alone by grace alone. But some false teachers came in, accusing Paul of distorting the true gospel and being dependent on Jerusalem. They sought to correct Paul and complete his gospel. They wanted to add the works of the Law, that which the Law requires, to the finished work of Christ for justification and transformation. Paul counters in two ways: one cannot be justified nor transformed by works of the Law because they are "works" and because they are "of the Old Covenant Law." Humanity in Adam is unable to keep the Law, and the Law is part of the old age.

Galatians is an eschatological letter from first to last. Now, I do not mean that it is concerned with the timeline of rapture/tribulation/millennium, but it is about the transition from Old Covenant to New Covenant, and the implications for the people of God. In other words, Galatians is about inaugurated eschatology, the fulfilment Jesus brings in his *first* coming.[45] The book is sandwiched by inaugurated eschatology, cross and kingdom. It begins and ends with the fact that through his cross, Jesus has ushered in the new age. The cross is the great exchange (the righteous for the unrighteous), as well as the great transition (from the Old Covenant to the New Covenant).[46] Galatians 1:4 says that Jesus "gave himself for our sins to deliver us from the present evil age." Great exchange: substitutionary atonement for our sins. Great transition: to deliver us from the present evil age. According to the Jewish worldview, history was divided into this age and the age to come. For them, the age to come was that future event where God

---

[45] See Benjamin L. Gladd and Matthew S. Harmon, *Making All Things New* (Grand Rapids: Baker Academic, 2016). I like G.K. Beale's definition of eschatology as "the movement toward the new-creational reign" in *A New Testament Biblical Theology* (Grand Rapids: Baker Academic, 2011), 23.

[46] Jeremy Treat, *The Crucified King* (Grand Rapids: Zondervan, 2014), 49. Treat's work is helpful in overcoming the all too common false dichotomies surrounding cross and kingdom.

would return (Isa 40-55), forgive their sin through the work of the Messiah (Jer 31, Isa 53), pour out his Spirit (Ezek 36, Joel 2), and raise his people from the dead (Ezek 37). Jesus yanks the future into the present through his person and work. He delivers us from the present age and places in the age to come. Now, we live in this overlap of the ages, between the already and not yet. Paul begins his letter with this glorious truth. The cross is the turning point of the ages.

Paul also ends the letter with this same truth. Galatians 6:14-15 says, "But far be it from me to boast except in the cross of our Lord Jesus Christ, by which the world has been crucified to me, and I to the world. For neither circumcision counts for anything, nor uncircumcision, but a new creation." Through the cross, the old age is crucified and the new creation has come.

What does all this have to do with the Sabbath? Everything, it turns out, because on the timeline of redemptive history, Paul places the Old Covenant Law on the "old age" side of the equation.[47] Law sides with Adam while Spirit sides with Christ. Part of being transferred to the new age is being freed from the Law. Galatians 3:15-29 is one of the clearest places in the New Testament regarding the temporary nature of the Old Covenant Law.[48] There,

---

[47] For the best singular treatment of Paul and the Law, see Rosner's careful work, *Paul and the Law*.

[48] John Murray was one of the leading advocates of Covenant Theology in his day. He was professor of New Testament Again, mad props to

Paul explicitly teaches that the Old Covenant Law had a definite starting point and a definite endpoint. He says the Law came 430 years *after* Abraham (Gal 3:17). It should go without saying, but if something has a starting point, it cannot be eternal. The Old Covenant Law was always meant to be a temporary stage in God's plan, a parenthetical placeholder to keep the nation of Israel together until the dawn of the new age. Notice the time marker Paul uses repeatedly. The Law was added *"until* the offspring should come" (Gal 3:19). It is not eternal but was given from the forming of the nation until the Messiah should come. The Law held people captive *"until* the coming faith would be revealed" (Gal 3:23). The Law was our guardian *until* Christ came (Gal 3:24).

Christ has come. Therefore, Jewish believers are no longer under the guardian. This word for "guardian" is *paidagōgos*. This word *does not* mean "tutor." Although we English speakers derive our word "pedagogue" from it, in the first century this word was distinct from tutor. The

---

Murray and the whole Westminster Philly tradition. Would that more modern pastors were reading Murray, Machen, and Van Til! But on this issue, I think the good doctor was off and as a proponent of Covenant Theology (especially of the mono-covenantal flavor), one would think he dealt with Galatians 3. Those who teach on covenantal continuities and discontinuities *must* handle Galatians 3! However, according to T. David Gordon, out of 221 reviews, articles, essays, and books, "not one of these addresses Galatians generally, nor a particular passage within Galatians specifically," "Abraham and Sinai Contrasted in Galatians 3:6-14," in *The Law Is Not of Faith: Essays on Works and Grace in the Mosaic Covenant,* Bryan D. Estelle, J. V. Fesko, and David VanDrunen, eds., (Phillipsburg, N.J: P & R Publishing, 2009), 253 n. 18.

guardian was more of a nanny than a teacher.[49] He was the domestic servant that took care of kids and was responsible to take the kids *to* the teacher. Here's the point: kids do not need nannies once they are full grown, which is precisely where Paul goes in chapter 4: a child is under a guardian *until* he grows up (Gal 4:1-4).[50]

New Covenant Christians are not under the guardian. Remember, the Sabbath was the sign of the Old Covenant. If it were to remain in force, Paul would need to make that crystal clear since he has taught so clearly that New Covenant believers are not bound to the Old Covenant Law. He would need to teach Gentiles about the

---

[49] Richard N. Longenecker, *Galatians* (Dallas: Word, 1990), 146; Douglas J. Moo, "The Law of Christ as the Fulfillment of the Law of Moses," in Stanley N. Gundry, eds., *Five Views on Law and Gospel* (Grand Rapids, Mich: Zondervan Academic, 1996), 338; Moo, "The Law or Moses or the Law of Christ," 214.

[50] On Galatians 3:25-26, John Chysostom writes, "The Law, then, as it was our tutor, and we were kept shut up under it, is not the adversary but the fellow-worker of grace. But if when grace is come it continues to hold us down, it becomes an adversary; for if it confines those who ought to go forward to grace, then it is the destruction of our salvation. If a candle which gave light by night kept us, when it became day, from the sun, it would not only not benefit, it would injure us. And so does the Law, if it stands between us and greater benefits. Those then are the greatest traducers of the Law who still keep it, just as the tutor makes a youth ridiculous by retaining him with himself when time calls for his departure," quoted in Longenecker, *Galatians,* li. Smells like New Covenant Theology in the 4th Century to me.

Sabbath and the necessity of keeping it. He is crystal clear that the opposite is the case.

Galatians 4:8-9 says, "Formerly, when you did not know God, you were enslaved to those that by nature are not gods. But now that you have come to know God, or rather to be known by God, how can you turn back again to the weak and worthless elementary principles of the world, whose slaves you want to be once more?" As the Galatian Christians are being tempted to revert to the ways of the old age, Paul warns them. "Remember, you used to be pagans, enslaved to the principalities and powers, in bondage to false gods. But you now know better. So how could you turn back to the elemental spirits of the world, to be enslaved all over again?" This is the same phrase that we saw in Colossians 2: the elemental spirits of the world.[51] In Colossians, it was to be enslaved by adding man-made rules to the gospel of Christ alone. Here, what is it? What are the Galatians doing that concerns Paul that they may be returning to enslavement?

Verses 10-11 say, "You observe days and months and seasons and years! I am afraid I may have labored over you in vain." Incredible. This is a staggering statement. Commentator C.K. Barrett writes, "Here in Galatians he virtually equates Judaism with heathenism. To go forward

---

[51] For some reason, the ESV translates the same phrase as "elemental spirits of the world" in Colossians, but as "elementary principles of the world" in Galatians. I think they got it right in Colossians, but off in Galatians.

into Judaism is to go backward into heathenism."[52] Once again, those who try to teach that the Old Covenant Sabbath is not in view here do not stand an exegetical chance.[53] The whole context of the letter is about the imposition of the Old Covenant Law on New Covenant

---

[52] C.K. Barrett, *Freedom and Obligation: A Study of the Epistle to the Galatians* (Philadelphia: Westminster, 1985), 61; So also Thomas R. Schreiner: "Apparently Paul equates living under the law with a reversion to paganism," *Galatians* (Grand Rapids: Zondervan, 2010): 276; "What is astonishing is that Paul equates subjection to Torah with paganism. One can only imagine the shock the Pauline assertion would have given the Judaizers," Ibid., 278; So also Longenecker: "Beyond question, Paul's lumping of Judaism and paganism together in this manner is radical in the extreme," *Galatians*, 181.

[53] John Frame acknowledges the difficulty for Sabbatarians. After grasping for straws at viable alternative readings to the plain sense, he says, "Of course, it is my Sabbatarian belief, taken from other parts of Scripture, that leads me to seek an exegesis of these passages [Gal 4, Col 2, Rom 14] compatible with continued Sabbath keeping," *The Doctrine of the Christian Life*, 571. Friends, I humbly submit that this is a bad way to do theology. Exegesis must drive our theology. We mustn't impose our theology onto Texts of Scripture. Huff as they might, these clear verses can't be blown down. Barcellos accuses me of making assertions about these texts in previous writings, "without much exegesis," *Getting the Garden Right*, 83. However, he devotes little space to these key passages. Quoting William Ames and John Owen do not amount to exegesis either. He really only dedicates four pages in a 272-page book to them (see 196, 204, 224-225) He asserts but does not establish the fact that the sabbaths mentioned in these verses do not include the Sabbath command of the Decalogue. For a better perspective, see Douglas J. Moo, *Galatians* (Grand Rapids: Baker Academic, 2013), 278; Schreiner, *Galatians*, 279.

believers.[54] Doubtless, the Jewish Sabbath would have been in view. Paul views their observing of the Jewish calendar as returning to the elemental spirits of the world, from which they have been freed. New Covenant Christians are not bound to keep the Sabbath. In fact, here, Paul *discourages* the practice as a means of pleasing God.

If the Sabbath were part of the eternal moral law of God, Paul would have been clearer to the Gentile churches. Not only does he never command Sabbath-keeping, he does just the opposite. The command to keep the Sabbath is not mentioned in Paul's letters and it was not mentioned at the Jerusalem Council in Acts 15, showing they and Paul were on the same page.[55] The Old Covenant Law was part of the old age and Christ has delivered us from the old age and "set us free" (Gal 5:1, 13). One cannot improve on the exhortation of Galatians 5:1: "For freedom Christ has set us

---

[54] Blomberg writes, "While again various pagan festivals might well fall under Paul's purview, references to Jewish holy days must be primary in his mind," "The Sabbath as Fulfilled in Christ," 348.

[55] This was the normal Jewish view. The Sabbath was for Jews, not for Gentiles. In fact, Jubilees 2:20 envisions a day when God will gather a people from the nations and thus will have "to make known to them the sabbath day so that they might observe therein a sabbath from all work." Jubilees 2:31 says, "The Creator of all blessed it, but he did not sanctify any people or nations to keep the sabbath thereon with the sole exception of Israel," James H. Charlesworth, ed., *The Old Testament Pseudepigrapha, Vol. 2: Expansions of the Old Testament and Legends, Wisdom and Philosophical Literature, Prayers, Psalms, and Odes, Fragments of Lost Judeo-Hellenistic Works*, 1st edition. (Garden City, NY: Doubleday and Company, 1985), 57.

free; stand firm therefore, and do not submit again to a yoke of slavery."

Chapter 9

Hebrews 4

~

The book of Hebrews is a sermon (Heb 13:22) exhorting and warning believers not to revert to the Old Covenant, but rather believe that Jesus is better and persevere to the end. Naturally, it has implications for a discussion on the Sabbath. The message could be summarized as "Jesus is better." Specifically, he is better than the Old Covenant. To make his case, the author, which I take to be Apollos (Acts 18:24-28) but that is neither here nor there, shows how the Old Testament points forward to Jesus and the covenant he would inaugurate by his shed blood. It is biblical theology par excellence. Sinclair Ferguson says Hebrews is "a key to the entire Bible, a road map to the whole history of redemption."[56]

Jesus is the pinnacle of divine revelation, as the first verse makes clear: "Long ago, at many times and in many ways, God spoke to our fathers by the prophets, but in these last days he has spoken to us by his Son, whom he appointed the heir of all things, through whom also he created the world." All previous revelation points to him and must be interpreted in light of him. At the transfiguration, we have the Law (Moses) and the Prophets (Elijah) present, but we are told to listen to the Son, and after the event, we are left with "Jesus only" (Matt 17:5-8).With Scripture, the key is found in the back of the book.

Hebrews 3:7-4:13 is the crucial passage for our purposes. I encourage you to give it a read before continuing to read this book. The author quotes from Psalm 95 to exhort the people to listen and not harden their hearts. Hebrews 3:11, quoting Psalm 95:11, says "As I swore in my wrath, they shall not enter my rest." He makes special mention of the fact that the Psalmist says "today." In Hebrews 3:16-19, he uses the Exodus generation as a negative example. Do not be like them. They did not listen. "Therefore, while the promise of entering his rest still stands, let us fear lest any of you should seem to have failed to reach it" (Heb 4:1). The promise of rest still stands. So listen!

---

[56] Sinclair Ferguson, *Christ Alone* (Orlando: Reformation Trust, 2007), 49.

"For we who have believed enter that rest, as he has said, 'As I swore in my wrath, they shall not enter my rest'" (Heb 4:3). We who have believed enter that promised rest. Seems clear enough, unless you are wearing confessional lenses. We obey the Sabbath by trusting Christ. As A.T. Lincoln puts it, "Therefore, the New Covenant people of God discharge their duty of Sabbath observance, according to this writer, by exercising faith."[57] Then he connects the rest of God with God's resting on the seventh day. Recall that that day was open-ended, and recall that in rabbinic Judaism, the new age was often described as "the world which is entirely Sabbath."[58] God's Sabbath rest – the way life is meant to be – is still available here and now as a foretaste of the consummated kingdom.

Verses 6-9 are crucial: "Since therefore it remains for some to enter it, and those who formerly received the good news failed to enter because of disobedience, again he

---

[57] A.T. Lincoln, "Sabbath, Rest, and Eschatology in the New Testament," in Carson, *From Sabbath to Lord's Day,* 213; similarly, Blomberg writes, "Because Jesus fulfilled the Law, and thus fulfilled the Sabbath command, He, not some day of the week, is what offers the believers rest. *We obey the Sabbath commandment of the Decalogue as we spiritually rest in Christ, letting Him bear our heavy burdens, trusting Him for salvation, and committing our lives to Him in service, then remaining faithful in lifelong loyalty to Him rather than committing apostasy,"* "The Sabbath as Fulfilled in Christ," 351.

[58] Lincoln, "Sabbath, Rest, and Eschatology in the New Testament," 199.

appoints a certain day, 'Today,' saying through David so long afterward, in the words already quoted, 'Today, if you hear his voice, do not harden your hearts.' For if Joshua had given them rest, God would not have spoken of another day later on. So then, there remains a Sabbath rest for the people of God."

For the writers of the New Testament, history matters. Chronology matters.[59] The Exodus generation did not enter rest. It remains for some today to enter that rest. Otherwise, David would never have mentioned a remaining rest in Psalm 95 "so long after" that Exodus generation. In other words, in the canonical narrative, Psalm 95 comes after Numbers 14. If Joshua had given true rest, there would have been no later promise of rest. Pretty straightforward. Read your Bible as a story and pay attention to the timeline. So the promise of Sabbath remains. Putting it together: Genesis 2 leaves seventh day rest open-ended, God promised rest to his people, they rebelled and did not enter it (Num 14:20-35), but Psalm 95 holds out the promise of true rest. So, believe (Heb 4:3)! Enter that rest by not reverting to the Old Covenant but trusting in the Messiah, the one greater than Moses (Heb 3:1-6). "For whoever has entered God's rest has also rested from his works as God did from his" (Heb 4:10). If Paul were writing, he would say

_____

[59] Consider how Paul argues the same way in Romans 4 and Galatians 3. It matters that Genesis 15 precedes Genesis 17. It matters that the Law came after Abraham and until the Messiah. In many ways, these writers are simply urging false teachers to go back and read the Bible as a story.

that we enter rest through justification by faith alone. We do not lean on our works or the works of the Law, but on Christ. The physical rest of the Old Covenant Sabbath has become spiritual rest in Christ. In the New Covenant era, to keep the Sabbath is to trust in Christ.

When the author commands us to strive to enter that rest, he does not mean that Sabbath rest is wholly future.[60] In Hebrews 4:10-11, the contrast of rest is damnation. Therefore, rest is salvation rest.[61] No one wants to posit that salvation is *wholly* future. That would be an *under*-realized eschatology. True and full eschatological rest is future, but we have a foretaste here and now through the full and final forgiveness of sins. Like every dimension of

---

[60] See A.T. Lincoln, "Sabbath, Rest, and Eschatology in the New Testament," 210-214; Thomas R. Schreiner, "Good-bye and Hello," 182-186; R.T. France, "Hebrews" in *The Expositor's Bible Commentary: Hebrews-Revelation,* eds., Tremper Longman III and David E. Garland (Grand Rapids: Zondervan, 2006); Donald Guthrie writes, "When he says, *we who have believed* (past tense) *enter* (present) *that rest,* he is stressing that the rest he is thinking of is an experience already in process of being fulfilled. It is not something simply to be hoped for in the future. It is an essential part of the present reality for Christians," *Hebrews* (Grand Rapids: Eerdmans, 1983), 112 (cf. 115-16). Even if one took the rest of Hebrews as wholly future, the argument for an enduring weekly Sabbath is still uncompelling in light of the canonical evidence.

[61] George Guthrie says, "The 'rest' of which the author of Hebrews speaks is entrance into the new covenant" in "Hebrews" in D. A. Carson and G. K. Beale, eds., *Commentary on the New Testament Use of the Old Testament* (Grand Rapids: Baker Academic, 2007), 960.

God's salvation, there is an already/not yet dimension to rest. We have it now but await its full consummation. As F.F. Bruce puts it, commenting on this verse, "by faith they may live in the good of it here and now."[62] To conclude that there is no Sabbath rest *today* from this passage misses the urgency of the warning. When we believe, we enter (*eiserchometha* – present tense) rest (Heb 4:3). The beauty of the gospel is that eschatological rest is a current reality for those in Christ, the firstborn from the dead.

Jesus brings a superior rest. Jesus is better, as the author of Hebrews pounds home again and again. Jewish tradition emphasized the fact that the Old Covenant Law came via angels (Heb 2:2, Gal 3:19, Acts 7:53) so Hebrews 1 shows the superiority of Jesus over angels. In chapter 7, the author shows that Jesus is a superior priest, because Melchizedek is superior to Abraham, and therefore Levi (Heb 7:1-10). Hebrews 7:11-12 says, "If perfection could have been attained through the Levitical priesthood—and indeed the law given to the people established that priesthood—why was there still need for another priest to come, one in the order of Melchizedek, not in the order of Aaron? For when the priesthood is changed, the law must be changed also" (NIV).[63] Here we learn about the structure

---

[62] F.F. Bruce, *The Epistle to the Hebrews* (Grand Rapids: Eerdmans, 1990), 110.

[63] In a rare miss, the ESV translates the genitives of Hebrews 7:12 as datives: "For when there is a change in the priesthood, there is necessarily a change in the law as well." The verse is not merely saying a

of the Old Covenant. The priesthood undergirds the Law, so that when one changes, the other does as well. Again, we see that the Law is a unit and cannot be divided into arbitrary parts. When the priesthood changes, the Law changes. New Covenant Christians do not have an Aaronic priest and are not under the Old Covenant Law.

We cannot move on from Hebrews without mentioning chapter 8. Jesus mediates a better covenant. The new covenant "is better, since it is enacted on better promises. For if that first covenant had been faultless, there would have been no occasion to look for a second" (Heb 8:6-7). One of the ways the preacher argues in Hebrews is by showing that the Old Testament itself pointed to its own obsolescence. The Old Testament Scriptures themselves point beyond itself. Here, Jeremiah 31 is the prophecy he is referring to. If all was good, if the Old Covenant Law had been eternal, there would have been no need and promise of a new covenant. He then quotes the longest Old Testament passage in the New Testament, Jeremiah 31:31-34. Then he closes the chapter with these words: "In speaking of a new covenant, he makes the first one obsolete. And what is becoming obsolete and growing old is ready to vanish away." The Old Covenant is now obsolete. In some ways, it was obsolete the day Jeremiah promised a new one, for there we see the Law's true purpose, to be "a shadow (*skia*) of the good things to come instead of the true

---

change in the priesthood and law, but *of* priesthood and law. One cannot help think that Covenant Theology presuppositions interpreted rather than translated on this one.

form of these realities" (Heb 10:1, Col 2:17).

Chapter 10

Christ Our Rest

~

So what? Does this debate really matter? Yes, for four reasons. First, it is an issue of authority. Will we let Scripture have the final and definitive word? I respect those who seek to ground their congregations in a confession, but when the confession betrays the Word of God, we must go with the Word, every time. This is merely applying the Reformation principle of *Sola Scriptura*. Tradition must be evaluated in light of Scripture (Mark 7:1-13). And, as has been shown, the New Testament is clear on the Sabbath. As New Testament scholar Richard Bauckham says, "Sabbatarian arguments have never succeeded in convincing all who sought to base their theology on the Protestant principle of *sola Scriptura.*[64]

Second, it matters because teachers of the Word will be held to a stricter judgment (James 3:1). It is vital that we interpret the Word rightly, especially when binding the consciences of God's people.[65] It matters that we get the Bible right. We do not want to miss the significance of Jesus and the changes he brings with the inauguration of the New Covenant. All previous Scripture must be interpreted in light of Jesus Christ.[66]

Third, we want to keep Jesus, not Law, central. The argument of this book has been that the Sabbath was meant to point the people of God to rest in Christ, not rest from physical work. To use Lutheran verbiage, the Sabbath should be gospel, not law. What are we pointing people to?

---

[64] R.J. Bauckham, "Sabbath and Sunday in the Protestant Tradition," in Carson, *From Sabbath to Lord's Day,* 312.

[65] The Baptist Faith and Message 2000 does a good job of reflecting the biblical teaching concerning the Lord's Day: "The first day of the week is the Lord's Day. It is a Christian institution for regular observance. It commemorates the resurrection of Christ from the dead and should include exercises of worship and spiritual devotion, both public and private. Activities on the Lord's Day should be commensurate with the Christian's conscience under the Lordship of Jesus Christ", Article VIII.

[66] This is the heart of New Covenant hermeneutics. Christ is central. *Everything* must be looked at through Jesus lenses. Contrary to Barcellos, who claims NCT "has yet to apply their basic hermeneutical principles consistently to this question." *Getting the Garden Right,* 271.

As Augustine put it, our hearts are restless until we find our rest in God. The people of God will not find rest by working six days and ceasing from work on one day. But, they will find rest in their Savior. We preach and teach the finished work of Christ and the Sabbath rest he provides. Jesus said, "Come to me, all who labor and are heavy laden, and I will give you rest. Take my yoke upon you, and learn from me, for I am gentle and lowly in heart, and you will find rest for your souls. For my yoke is easy, and my burden is light" (Matt 11:28-30). *He,* not another command, is what the people of God need. Matthew has an unfortunate chapter break between eleven and twelve, because right after Jesus invites us to find our rest in him, Matthew tells the story of the disciples plucking heads of grain on the Sabbath where the narrative ends with the declaration that "The Son of Man is lord of the Sabbath" (Matt 12:8). *He* is the point of the Sabbath.

Fourth, we need to be a people who sanctify *every day* to the Lord. Not one, but all seven days are His. Worship is all of life (Rom 12:1). This is not to say the corporate gathering of the church is not important. It is! Vitally so. And the first day is important too.[67] I believe New Testament churches should do all they can to gather on the Lord's Day, the first day of the week, in honor of the resurrection of Jesus. This is not the same thing as saying the seventh day is now the first day. As has been shown,

---

[67] Barcellos spends pages 211-230 on the importance of the first day, *Getting the Garden Right.* One can affirm the importance of gathering on the first day without Sabbatarianism.

that is a category mistake. No text of Scripture teaches that the Lord's Day is now the Christian Sabbath. Transfer theology is not grounded in exegesis, but tradition.

This is not to say that rest is unimportant either. With our hectic, always-connected culture, it is as important as ever. This is why there has been a resurgence of writing on the "Sabbath" from non-Sabbatarian circles. It seems that most of them are not actually engaging biblical teaching but reacting to the pace of life of modern America. Many Americans need to disconnect and rest. Those made in the image of God ought to be good stewards of their God-given bodies. We need to disconnect from work. I prefer the modern five-day work week to the Old Covenant six-day work week. Smartphone usage needs to be minimized. Vacation days should be used. Sleep should be had. Yes and amen. But these sorts of wisdom-based exhortations are not the same as the Old Covenant command to keep the Sabbath holy.

Chapter 11

Conclusion

~

Christians are not bound to the Sabbath command. The Sabbath command is not a creation ordinance. The Sabbath was never changed by God from Saturday to Sunday. There is no tripartite division of the Old Covenant Law. Several New Testament passages are crystal clear that Christians are not bound to the Old Covenant Law, including the command to work six days and rest on Saturday.

The seventh day at creation, and the later Sabbath command pointed forward to something greater. To the One who alone brings true rest. Here and now, we can rest from our works by trusting in the Messiah. We can have a taste of the life to come in the present evil age. In the New Covenant, to obey the Sabbath is to trust King Jesus. Rest in Him

Bibliography

1689 Federalism Compared to New Covenant Theology &
Progressive Covenantalism, Accessed December 24,
2019.
https://www.youtube.com/watch?v=_Uq_S3-
HjRo.

Ascol, Thomas K. *From the Protestant Reformation to the*
Southern Baptist Convention: What Hath Geneva to Do
with Nashville. 2nd edition. Cape Coral, FL: Founders
Press, 2013.

Barcellos, Richard. *In Defense of the Decalogue : A Critique of*
New Covenant Theology. Enumclaw, WA: Winepress
Publishing, 2001.

Barrett, C.K. *Freedom and Obligation: A Study of the Epistle to*
the Galatians. Philadelphia: Westminster, 1985.

Bruce, F.F. *The Epistle to the Hebrews.* Grand Rapids:
Eerdmans, 1990.

Carson, D. A., ed. *From Sabbath to Lord's Day: A Biblical,*
Historical and Theological Investigation. Eugene, OR:
Wipf & Stock Pub, 2000.

Carson, D. A., and G. K. Beale, eds. *Commentary on the New Testament Use of the Old Testament.* Grand Rapids: Baker Academic, 2007.

Charlesworth, James H., ed. *The Old Testament Pseudepigrapha, Vol. 2: Expansions of the Old Testament and Legends, Wisdom and Philosophical Literature, Prayers, Psalms, and Odes, Fragments of Lost Judeo-Hellenistic Works.* 1st edition. Garden City, N.Y: Doubleday and Company, 1985.

Donato, Christopher John. *Perspectives on the Sabbath: Four Views.* Nashville, TN: B&H Academic, 2011.

Estelle, Bryan D., J. V. Fesko, and David VanDrunen, eds. *The Law Is Not of Faith: Essays on Works and Grace in the Mosaic Covenant.* Phillipsburg, NJ: P&R Publishing, 2009.

Feinberg, John S., ed. *Continuity and Discontinuity: Perspectives on the Relationship Between the Old and New Testaments.* Wheaton, IL: Crossway, 1988.

France, R.T. "Hebrews." In *The Expositor's Bible Commentary: Hebrews-Revelation.* Grand Rapids: Zondervan, 2006.

Frame, John M. *The Doctrine of the Christian Life.* Phillipsburg, N.J: P&R Publishing, 2008.

Gentry, Peter J., and Dr Stephen J. Wellum. *Kingdom Through Covenant: A Biblical-Theological Understanding of the*

Covenants. 1st edition. Wheaton, IL: Crossway
    Books, 2012.

George, Timothy and Denise George, eds. *Baptist Confessions,*
    Covenants, and Catechisms. Nashville: B&H, 1996.

Gundry, Stanley, ed. *Five Views on Law and Gospel.* Grand
    Rapids: Zondervan Academic, 1996.

Howson, Barry Hamlin. "A Historical and Comparative
    Study of the First and Second London Baptist
    Confessions of Faith with Reference to the
    Westminster and Savoy Confessions." M.A., McGill
    University (Canada), 1996.

Kendall, Heather A. *One Greater Than Moses: A History of New*
    Covenant Theology. Orange, CA: Quoir, 2016.

Long, Gary D. *The First London Confession of Faith, 1646*
    Edition: With an Appendix by Benjamin Cox. North
    Charleston, SC: BookSurge Publishing, 2003.

Longenecker, Richard N. *Galatians.* Dallas: Word, 1990.

Lucas, R. C. *The Message of Colossians and Philemon.* Downers
    Grove, IL: IVP Academic, 1984.

Lumpkin, W.L. *Baptist Confessions of Faith.* Valley Forge:
    Judson Press, 1974.

Lumpkin, William L. *The Story of Baptist Confessions of Faith.*
    Louisville: The Southern Baptist Theological

Seminary, 1957.

Luther, Martin. *Commentary on Romans*. Grand Rapids: Kregel, 1954.

McGlothlin, W.J. *Baptist Confessions of Faith*. Philadelphia: American Baptist Publication Society, 1911.

Moo, Douglas J. *Galatians*. Grand Rapids, MI: Baker Academic, 2013.

_____. *The Epistle to the Romans*. Twelfth Impression edition. Grand Rapids, Mich: Eerdmans, 1996.

_____. *The Letters to the Colossians and to Philemon*. Grand Rapids: Eerdmans, 2008.

Pao, David W. *Colossians and Philemon*. Grand Rapids: Zondervan, 2012.

Reeves, Stan, ed. *The 1689 Baptist Confession of Faith in Modern English*. Cape Coral, Florida: Founders Press, 2017.

Reisinger, John G. *Abraham's Four Seeds*. Frederick, MD: New Covenant Media, 1998.

_____. *The Believer's Sabbath*. Frederick, MD: New Covenant Media, 2002.

Rosner, Brian S., T. Desmond Alexander, Graeme Goldsworthy, and D. A. Carson, eds. *New Dictionary of Biblical Theology: Exploring the Unity Diversity of Scripture*. Downers Grove, IL: IVP Academic, 2000.

Schreiner, Thomas. *40 Questions About Christians and Biblical Law*. Grand Rapids, MI: Kregel Academic & Professional, 2010.

Stott, John. *The Message of Romans: God's Good News for the World*. Leicester, England ; Downers Grove, IL: IVP Academic, 2001.

Wellum, Dr Stephen J., and Brent E. Parker, eds. *Progressive Covenantalism: Charting a Course between Dispensational and Covenantal Theologies*. Nashville: B&H Academic, 2016.

Wenkel, David H. *The London Baptist Confession of 1646: A Modern Version for the Church Today*. Greenville, SC: Emerald House Group, Incorporated, 2017

White, A. Blake. *The Law of Christ: A Theological Proposal*. Frederick, MD: New Covenant Media, 2010.

———. *The Newness Of The New Covenant*. Frederick, MD: New Covenant Media, 2007.

———. *What Is New Covenant Theology? An Introduction*. Frederick, MD: New Covenant Media, 2012.

Made in the USA
Las Vegas, NV
30 April 2021